IRISH DANCING

AND OTHER NATIONAL DANCES

RITA STOREY

W

FRANKLIN WATTS
LONDON • SYDNEY

IRISH DANCING
AND OTHER NATIONAL DANCES

A national dance is a dance associated with a particular country. It is often a folk dance that has been adopted as a symbol of the country's culture and history – for example lively Irish dancing, passionate Spanish flamenco, or the beautiful and delicate dances of India.

National dances are often performed at important international events such as the opening of the Olympic Games. Because events like this are broadcast all over the world, the dances are seen by a huge audience. People become interested in learning the national dances of other countries. Irish dancing became very popular after it was shown during the 1994 Eurovision Song Contest, which was held in Dublin, Ireland.

Why should *I* dance?

Dancing is good for everyone. It's a great way to get fit. All types of dancing are a form of aerobic exercise, which encourages your heart and lungs to work hard. Over time, this will help them to become stronger and make *you* fitter.

The food we eat provides our body with the energy it needs to work properly. But if we eat more calories than our body needs, these are stored as fat. Dancing makes your body burn off calories. Your muscles will strengthen and become firmer, and your body will become more shapely.

Dancing makes you happy

When you take exercise, your brain makes a hormone called seratonin, which makes you feel happy. So if you're feeling miserable, put down the chocolate, put on the music and start dancing.

There are so many types of dance that there really is something for everyone. You can do the dance moves in this book on your own or with a friend, and work at a pace that suits you.

Dancing can even boost your brain power. Putting together dance steps increases your coordination and helps keep your mind alert.

Last but not least, dancing is fun. So what are you waiting for? Turn up the music and get moving!

Contents

Let's get moving

Why do I have to warm up?

Before you learn any new dance steps and begin to put them together, it is important to warm up your muscles to prevent cramp and muscle strain. You may only be able to do the exercises a couple of times to start with, but persevere and do a few more repeats each time. A warm-up should last about ten minutes.

There are warm-up moves in each of the four books in the Get Dancing series. You can combine them to make a routine.

Aerobic exercises

The first set of exercises is aerobic, which means that it improves your breathing and circulation. Aerobic exercise increases your oxygen intake by making your heart beat faster. To do it, you have to keep on the move all the time. Each set of aerobic exercises is designed to be repeated. If you are not used to exercise and feel your pulse starting to race, stop and jog on the spot to keep warm.

AEROBIC EXERCISE

RUNNING ON THE SPOT

Run on the spot. Start by running for 25 counts (count one when both feet have touched the floor). When that seems really easy, add another block of 25.

VARIATION
After running for a count of 50, do 5 jumps straight up in the air (keeping both feet together).

ISOLATION
SHOULDER

1 With your fingers resting on your shoulders, roll your shoulders forward, so that your elbows make a big circle.

2 With your fingers resting on your shoulders, roll your shoulders backwards, so that your elbows make a big circle.

Repeat 4 times.

Body isolations

The second set of exercises is a body isolation. This type of exercise teaches you to move parts of your body individually, which is important for all types of dancing.

What to wear

Wear something comfortable to do a warm-up, such as loose-fitting trousers (not jeans), a T-shirt, and a loose, long-sleeved top that you can take off when you have warmed up.

You can do the routine in bare feet, trainers or jazz shoes. Don't do it in socks, or you may slip.

Dance to the music

You will need at least two pieces of music for the warm-up. The first is for the aerobic exercises. It should be energetic and upbeat, to make everyone feel enthusiastic. It can also be used for body isolations, which are sharp, quick moves.

The second piece of music will be used for the stretches and toning exercises (see page 6). Gentle, relaxing music is best for this part of the warm-up.

Let's get moving

Stretches

The most important thing to remember about stretches is that they should be done gradually. It's easy to pull a muscle by pushing yourself too hard, too soon.

Try doing the exercises every day and stretching just a little bit further each time. If it hurts, STOP. You may feel a bit stiff the next day if you haven't been exercising regularly, but you shouldn't be in pain. If you are, you have stretched too hard – stop for a few days and then start building up the stretches slowly.

Toning exercises

These exercises are to strengthen and tone particular muscles, giving you a better body shape and strong muscles to hold the dance moves.

STRETCH AND TONE

HAMSTRING STRETCH

1 Sit on the floor with your legs as wide apart as you can. Stretch your body over your right leg, getting your nose as close to your knee as you can manage.

2 Stretch out straight in front of you whilst touching each foot, getting your nose as close to the floor as you can. Keep your back straight.

3 Stretch your body over your left leg, getting your nose as close to your knee as you can manage.

Hold each position for a slow count of 10.

Cool it!

At the end of a dance session, it is important to do a cool-down routine to help prevent stiffness the next day. The routine concentrates on stretching exercises that stretch out and relax the muscles. To be effective, each stretch should be held for a slow count of ten. A cool-down routine should last for five to ten minutes.

Each of the four books in the Get Dancing series contains cool-down stretches. You can use a combination from different books if you wish.

Hold each move for a slow count of 10.

COOL IT! 1
THIGH STRETCH

COOL IT! 2
ARM STRETCH

1 Stand with your feet apart. Interlock your fingers, and with your palms facing upwards, stretch your arms up as high as you can.

1 Standing with your feet together, bring your knee up to your chest and hug it tight.

2 Repeat with the other knee.

7

Irish dancing

There are different kinds of Irish dancing: step dancing, ceili dancing, and set dancing.

Step dancing

Step dancing is a fast, high-kicking style of dancing, which is performed as a solo dance or a group dance. It is danced with the arms held rigidly by the sides. Irish step dancers often enter competitions called feis (pronounced 'fesh'). There are local, regional, national and world feis. Step dances consist of jigs, reels and hornpipes.

Ceili dancing

Ceili dancing (pronounced 'kaylee') is Irish folk dancing. It is done in groups, the steps are easy to pick up, and people dance it just for fun.

Set dancing

Set dancing is done in groups, using step-dancing moves.

A step-dancing dress worn for performing.

What to wear for step dancing

Practice clothes

Soft shoes (like ballet shoes) or hard tap shoes are worn.

Girls wear clothes that allow them to do high kicks: a short, full skirt or shorts. These are worn with a blouse with loose sleeves, or a T-shirt. Boys also wear a shirt with full sleeves or a T-shirt, and trousers or a kilt.

Performance clothes

For competitions, girls wear short, embroidered dresses. These are often made of heavy velvet and decorated with lots of Irish symbols. Girls often wear their hair in ringlets.

For some dances, soft shoes are worn. Girls' soft shoes are called gillies. These are like ballet shoes but with intricate lacing at the front. For other dances, hard shoes are needed. Girls' hard shoes have a metal plate on the heel and the toe.

Boys wear kilts or black trousers, blazers, ties, waistcoats and hard or soft shoes.

RIVERDANCE

Stealing the show

In 1994, the Eurovision Song Contest was held in Dublin, Ireland. During a break between songs, a troupe of dancers performed a short step-dancing routine called 'Riverdance'. An audience of 300 million television viewers saw the beauty, grace and excitement of Irish step dancing, and this ensured its future popularity.

The dance routine included traditional and modern music, and hard-shoe step dancing. The lead dancer, Michael Flatley, and Jean Butler, his female co-star, gave an unforgettable performance. The audience was captivated and some people thought it was the highlight of the Eurovision Song Contest.

Riverdance – the stage show

The response to the seven minutes of 'Riverdance' was so positive that plans were made to create a stage show. In 1995, *Riverdance* opened as a two-hour-long show, with Michael Flatley and Jean Butler again dancing the lead roles.

Irish history

The *Riverdance* stage show explores the history of Ireland and its people through music, song and dance. Most of the dancing is soft-shoe and hard-shoe Irish step dancing, but there are elements of Spanish, Russian and African dance in it as well. These are there to reflect all the cultures that make up Ireland today.

The cast of the *Riverdance* stage show performing at the Apollo Theatre, London.

Feet of flames

Basic steps in Irish step dancing

There are three basic types of step: threes, sevens and jig steps.

Threes

The three-step can consist of jumps, hops or kicks. It is used to dance in one place, or move forwards or backwards. To dance the jump threes step, you dance from your right foot to your left foot to your right foot. Then you dance from your left foot to your right foot to your left foot. Lift your knees high as you dance.

JUMP THREES

2 Kick your front (right) leg in the air, keeping it straight, with toes pointed.

1 Starting position: feet together, with the heel of the right foot by the toes of the left foot.

3 Jump off the back (left) foot on to the front (right) foot.
As you do this, kick your back foot up and kick your bottom.
As you land, put your back (left) foot down at the front. You should now be back in the basic position, but with the left foot in front.

HOP THREES

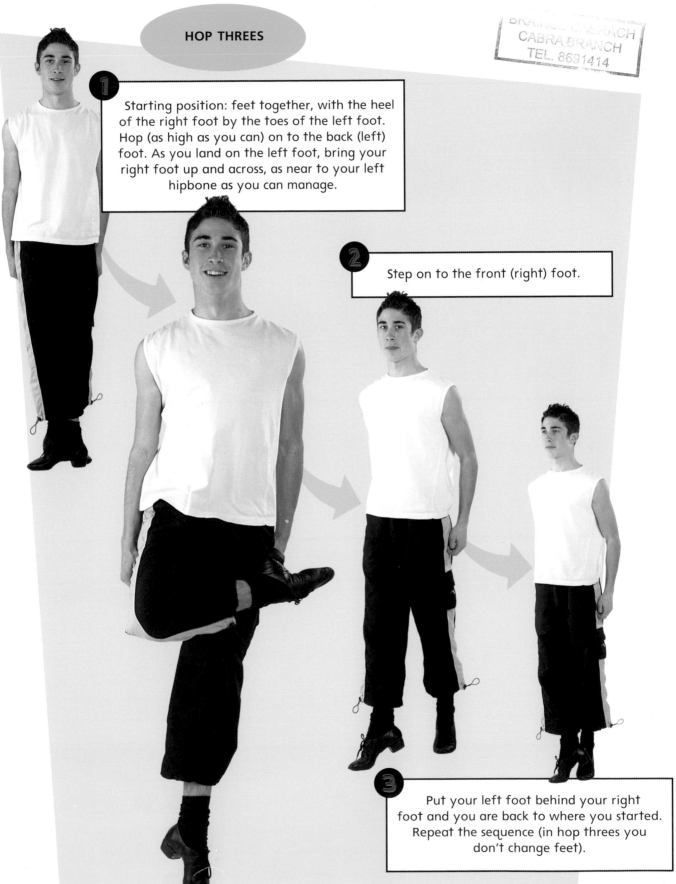

1 Starting position: feet together, with the heel of the right foot by the toes of the left foot. Hop (as high as you can) on to the back (left) foot. As you land on the left foot, bring your right foot up and across, as near to your left hipbone as you can manage.

2 Step on to the front (right) foot.

3 Put your left foot behind your right foot and you are back to where you started. Repeat the sequence (in hop threes you don't change feet).

Feet of flames

Sevens

The seven step is a travelling step used when you want to dance to the side. When dancing sevens, you are moving in the direction of the foot that is in front. The front foot stays in front.

SEVENS
MOVING TO THE LEFT

1 Starting position: feet together, with the heel of the left foot by the toes of the right foot.
Hop on the back (right) foot. Bring your left foot up as high as you can towards your hipbone (see page 11). You won't be able to do this straight away. Start by bringing your foot up to knee height and try to get it a bit higher each time you practise.

2 Jump on to your front (left) foot, placing it in front and to the left of the right foot.

3 Cross your back (right) foot behind your left foot, and hop on to it.

Body positions for Irish step dancing

When step dancing, always remember to keep your arms straight by your sides. Your hands should be closed into a fist, with your thumb tucked inside.

Keep your head up, with your neck straight and your shoulders back.

Keep your feet in a pointed position. Never turn up your toes so that you show the sole of your foot. Lift your knees high as you dance.

4 Jump on to your front (left) foot, placing it in front and to the left of the right foot.

5 Cross your back (right) foot behind your left foot, and hop on to it.

6 Jump on to your front (left) foot, placing it in front and to the left of the right foot.

7 Cross your back (right) foot behind your left foot, and hop on to it.

VARIATION
You can repeat this sequence to move further to the left. Or, to move back the other way, bring your back (right) foot to the front, as high towards your hipbone as you can. Then, keeping this foot in front, dance the rest of the steps to the right.

Jig step

This jig step is a travelling step, where you move forwards and change feet. It combines the jump threes and the hop threes described on pages 10–11.

Dance to the music

Riverdance (composer Bill Whelan). *Lord of The Dance* (composer Ronan Hardiman). *Feet of Flames* (composer Ronan Hardiman). Mike Shaffer: *Dance to the Music – Traditional Irish Dance Music*. Pat King: *Three Score and Ten.*

JIG STEP

1 Starting position: feet together, with the heel of the left foot by the toes of the right foot.
Hop on the back (right) foot. Bring your left foot up as high as you can towards your hipbone (see page 11). You won't be able to do this straight away. Start by bringing your foot up to knee height and try to get it a bit higher each time you practise.

2 Jump on to your front (left) foot, placing it in front and to the left of the right foot.

3 Cross your back (right) foot behind your front (left) foot, and hop on to it.

4 Hop on your front (left) foot, kicking your back (right) foot up behind you.

5 Put your back (right) foot to the front, placing it in front and to the right of the left foot.

VARIATION
Repeat the moves with the opposite feet.

VARIATION
Once you've done the jig step, try combining some of the basic steps. Do jump threes twice, then sevens to the right, sevens to the left, and hop threes twice. Repeat from the beginning.

Skilled dancers

Experienced Irish step dancers have a special way of changing their weight from one side of the body to the other (shown right). Don't try it yourself: it takes a lot of practice to be able to perform it without hurting your feet.

Spanish flamenco

The flamenco rhythm

Spanish flamenco dancing is danced to an uneven, twelve-beat rhythm. This can make it difficult to dance, as most of the dances that we are used to are danced to a regular beat. The rhythm of flamenco is counted with the emphasis on the third, sixth, eighth, tenth and twelfth beat.

1 2 **3** 4 5 **6** 7 **8** 9 **10** 11 **12**

Counting the rhythm

Count out loud from one to twelve. Say the numbers **3**, **6**, **8**, **10** and **12** louder than the rest. Can you hear the rhythm?

Clapping the rhythm

Now clap your hands while you count. Clap harder on beats **3**, **6**, **8**, **10** and **12**.

Stamping the rhythm

First stamp your left foot and then your right foot, twelve times, stamping harder on beats **3**, **6**, **8**, **10** and **12**.

Dancing the rhythm

Now count the beats one to twelve in your head and stamp and clap at the same time, stamping and clapping louder on beats **3**, **6**, **8**, **10** and **12**.

Hold your hands up high as you clap. Can you feel yourself flamenco dancing already?

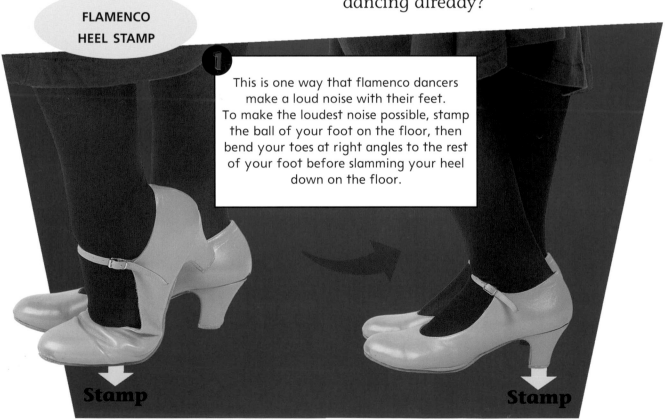

FLAMENCO HEEL STAMP

This is one way that flamenco dancers make a loud noise with their feet. To make the loudest noise possible, stamp the ball of your foot on the floor, then bend your toes at right angles to the rest of your foot before slamming your heel down on the floor.

Stamp   Stamp

FLAMENCO
FOOT STAMP

Another way to make a loud noise with your feet is to stamp the whole of your foot on the floor. To do this in flamenco dancing, you kick your leg up behind you and stamp it down. You must do this without bringing your knee forwards.

Stamp

FLAMENCO
HAND CLAPPING

Standing tall

It is important to stand correctly before you begin. Shoulders should be relaxed and pulled back, back straight, and head held high. Your knees should be slightly bent and your weight should all be in the lower half of your body. This feels strange at first, but as you start to tap and stamp your feet, it becomes quite natural.

Hand clapping

The Spanish word for the hand clapping in flamenco is 'palmas'. Palmas is either loud or soft.

To clap loudly, hold your left hand up to head height, cup the palm and hit it with the middle three fingers of your right hand. When this is done correctly, it makes a sharp, loud clap. To clap softly, cup the fingers of both hands and clap them together to make a gentler sound.

Spanish flamenco

Arms and hands

One of the most characteristic things about flamenco dancing is the way that the girls use their arms. The arms are held up high, in a gentle curve, so that the elbows do not stick out. The hands are then turned from the wrist to make the dance movements.

FLAMENCO STEP SEQUENCE

Stamp

Stamp

1 Starting position: feet together, arms at waist height, crossed at the wrists with the palms facing up.
Stamp with the right foot, counting the beats as you do so. Stamp first with the ball of your foot (on count 1), then heel (on count 2), then the whole foot (on count 3).
As you make each move, gradually bring your arms up higher.
1 2 **3**

2 Stamp the ball of your left foot (on count 4).
4

Stamp

Spanish flamenco

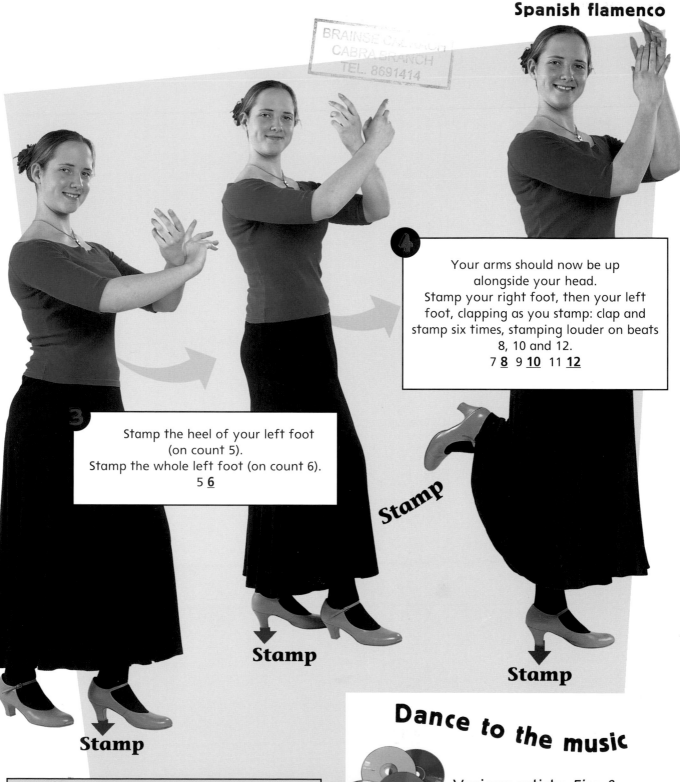

4
Your arms should now be up alongside your head.
Stamp your right foot, then your left foot, clapping as you stamp: clap and stamp six times, stamping louder on beats 8, 10 and 12.
7 **8** 9 **10** 11 **12**

3
Stamp the heel of your left foot (on count 5).
Stamp the whole left foot (on count 6).
5 **6**

Stamp

Stamp

Stamp

Stamp

Stamp

VARIATION
This sequence may seem very simple, but the flamenco tempo is very fast. Start slowly and then speed up. Roll your hands over each other, keeping your wrists together.

Dance to the music

Various artists: *Fire & Passion: The New Flamenco*. Paco Pena: *Fabulous Flamenco*. Various artists: *The Rough Guide to Flamenco*.

What to wear

Practice clothes

Girls require flamenco shoes, which are made of suede or leather, with a heel of 3–5 cm (1–2 in) high. They have little pieces of metal on the heel and toes, for tapping out the rhythms of the dance. Alternatively, tap shoes can be worn.

Girls also need a practice skirt. This should be long, and either plain or with ruffles. It is worn with a vest or jersey called a maillot (a close-fitting T-shirt would be a good substitute).

Boys wear plain trousers and a T-shirt. They also wear shoes with metal on the heel and toe.

Performance clothes

For dancing at festivals, girls wear a traditional flamenco dress. This is long, with ruffles on the skirt and sleeves. Large coloured flowers are pinned in the hair, which is usually worn in a bun.

For dancing on stage, the style of dress is simpler, using flowing shapes rather than ruffles.

Traditionally, boys used to wear high-waisted trousers, shirts with frills, and a short jacket with a sash. That has now changed and modern flamenco dancers wear plain trousers and a shirt in dark colours.

Accessories

Expert flamenco dancers use props to perform some of their dances. These include a shawl (*manton*), a fan (*pericon*), and castanets (*castañuelas*). Castanets are wooden discs that are clicked together in time to the music.

A famous modern flamenco dancer, Joaquim Cortes, dancing in his show *Soul*. Many flamenco dance performances today are done in simple costumes that make it easy to see the movements of the body.

THE SPIRIT OF FLAMENCO

Gypsy dance

Flamenco is the most famous of Spain's traditional dances. It was invented by gypsies (*flamencos*) in Andalusia in southern Spain. This type of dancing is danced on a hard floor, with hard shoes, and is very rhythmic.

Flamenco style

Flamenco is made up of three things: song (*canto*), dance (*baile*), and guitar-playing (*guitarra*). Men and women dance different steps. Men do intricate toe-and-heel-clicking steps, whilst the women's dance has more graceful hand and body movements.

Music

Flamenco dances are traditionally accompanied by Spanish guitar and a pair of castanets – which the dancers often play themselves. The dances also involve clapping, foot stamping and shouting to the beat of the music.

There are dozens of different forms of flamenco, and within each form there are many variations. Different areas of Spain have their own particular styles of the dance.

Expressing feelings

As well as basic steps, flamenco dancing involves improvisation. Each dancer uses the dance to express his or her feelings about things such as love, hate, pride, sorrow and joy. A really good flamenco dancer has what the Spanish call *duende* (pronounced 'dwen-day') – a special inner feeling that inspires the dancer to great performances.

Fiestas

In Spain, people enjoy big outdoor parties called fiestas. In Seville there is a huge fiesta every spring, which goes on all day and all night. A million people take part in the fun. All around Seville, tents of brightly coloured canvas are set up to use as dance halls. There is music and flamenco dancing, and everyone is encouraged to join in. Many of the women wear colourful gypsy flamenco dresses.

To dance flamenco, you need to stand very upright and look proud and confident.

Indian dancing

Indian dancing is quite complicated. As well as learning the steps, you also need to learn the correct rhythms and postures. Indian dance is a blend of three things: *nritta*, *nrity* and *natya*.

Nritta is the body movements made to the rhythms of a dance.

Nrity is the combination of rhythm and expression. It is shown through the eyes, hands and facial expression.

Natya is the storytelling element of a dance, when the dance is used to depict an Indian legend.

Bharata natyam

One classical form of Indian dancing is bharata natyam, which is traditionally danced by women.

Before each session, the dancer recites a prayer to the Earth to apologise for stamping on the ground, as the dances involve beating a rhythm on the ground with bare feet.

Traditionally, bharata natyam takes seven years to learn because it is so complicated. It has 120 basic steps called *adavus*, made up of poses and movements. Some are shown on pages 22 to 26 for you to try out and perhaps use in your own dances.

This is one of a group of bharata natyam adavus called nattadavu, which are stretching movements.

NATTADAVU 1

CLASSICAL INDIAN DANCING

Classical Indian dances are amongst the most graceful in the world. However, learning Indian dance is rather like trying to learn a new language, as combinations of movements of the feet, knees, hips, arms, legs, hands, head and eyes can mean different things.

There are six major classical dances, each of which developed in a different region of India. They were all originally devotional dances to various gods. The six dances are:

kathakali and mohiniyattam,
bharata natyam,
kuchipudi,
odissi,
manipuri,
kathak.

Two of these classical styles are still very popuar today – kathak and bharata natyam.

Kathak
Kathak comes from northern India. This style of dance tells a story. Originally, it was danced by people called kathakas, who told stories from history while entertaining people with dance, mime and music. Kathak involves fast, whirling movements.

Bharata natyam
This style of dance comes from southern India. 'Bharata' is made up of three words, which stand for emotion, melody and rhythm. 'Natyam' means the art of dance.

The 120 adavus (basic steps) in bharata natyam split into two types: poses (*sthanakas*) and movements (*charis*). These elements have to be learnt before any actual dancing starts. Then they are combined into groups of steps (*jethis*), then sequences (*thirmanams*), and finally into whole dances.

The hand movements in bharata natyam have special meanings.

23

Indian dancing

Sarikkal adavus are a series of sliding moves with the feet ('*sarikkal*' means 'to slide') combined with intricate arm and hand movements.

Mai adavus are moves that use the flexibility of the whole body ('*mai*' means 'body').

SARIKKAL ADAVU

The nine emotions

In Indian dancing, you learn to display nine emotions or *navrasas*, which are expressed by the eyes, the face and the body, and are common to all classical Indian dance. The emotions are: happiness (*hasya*), anger (*krodha*), disgust (*bhibasta*), fear (*bhaya*), sorrow (*shoka*), courage (*viram*), wonder (*adbhuta*), serenity (*shanta*), and compassion (*karuna*).

East meets West

You might like to try blending some of the adavus with modern Western dance steps to create an exciting and original dance routine, just like they do in Bollywood films (see page 27). Combine lots of influences, such as hip-hop dance steps and modern tap.

MAI ADAVU

24

What to wear

Hindu temple dancers

The dances of bharata natyam have a long history.

Originally they would have been danced by women who dedicated their lives to the Hindu religion and were considered to be married to the gods. They were called the handmaids of the gods, or *devadasis*. The devadasis would dance in the temples as part of religious ceremonies.

Costume

The history of bharata natyam is reflected in the outfits worn by girls who dance it today. They wear a costume that is designed to resemble a Hindu temple sculpture. As these

A dancer wearing a traditional bharata natyam costume.

sculptures are frequently decorated with flowers and ornaments, the costumes often include flowers and jewellery.

Clothes to move in

The costume may be a dress, or a top and a pair of loose trousers. Dresses are pleated at the front to allow ease of movement. If trousers are worn, a pleated section called a *pallu* is attached to the front.

Feet

The dances are performed in bare feet. Dancers often decorate their feet by painting on intricate designs with a dye called henna. Anklets with rows of bells are worn to add a musical accompaniment to the moves.

25

One group of adavus is called nattadavu (see also page 22). These are stretching movements. In the adavu shown here, the left leg is stretched out, with the heel striking the floor. The foot is then brought back alongside the right foot and stamped. The movement is repeated with the right leg.

Dance to the music

Cultural Centre of India: *Dances of India – Bharata Natyam Songs*. Various artists: *The Best of Bollywood*. The orginal London cast of *Bombay Dreams*: *Bombay Dreams*.

NATTADAVU 2

BOLLYWOOD

Many people have come to know classical Indian dance because of the popularity of Indian musical films all around the world.

The Indian film industry is one of the biggest in the world, and many of the films are an exciting and colourful mix of music, dancing, songs and comedy. The films blend different classical Indian dance styles with Western dance steps.

Bollywood films

Most Indian films are made in the city of Mumbai, which has been nicknamed Bollywood. This is a combination of the words 'Hollywood' (the famous centre of film-making in the USA) and 'Bombay' (the old name for Mumbai).

Bollywood films have made people much more aware of Indian dance, and dance classes in kathak and bharata natyam are becoming very popular in many countries.

Bombay Dreams

In 2002, a stage musical called *Bombay Dreams* opened in London. The musical was produced by Andrew Lloyd Webber. He created a Bollywood-style show full of songs and dance routines, using a cast of Asian performers.

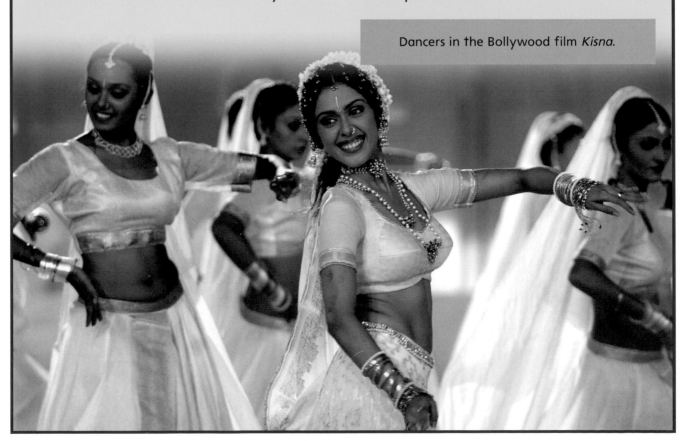

Dancers in the Bollywood film *Kisna*.

Other national dances

National dances help give people a sense of belonging. Sometimes, countries go through difficult times. If a country is occupied by people with a different cultural background as a result of war, the traditions of the resident population may be suppressed. At times like this especially, traditional songs and dances help people to remember their own culture and identity.

The samba

The Brazilians hold a huge festival in spring, called the carnival. It is one of the biggest festivals in the world today. In Brazil's largest city, Rio de Janeiro, the streets come alive with people dressed in exotic costumes dancing the samba.

The carnival was originally a religious festival, which people celebrated before fasting for forty days over Lent.

The samba comes from African culture. The dance became part of the carnival in the early 1900s when a large number of black Brazilians moved to the slums of Rio after the abolition of slavery in Brazil.

The haka

The haka is a Maori war dance from New Zealand. It was performed to get warriors into top physical condition to fight a battle.

Today, the haka has been adopted as a pre-match battle dance by the All Blacks, New Zealand's national rugby team (see page 30 for details of a website that tells you how to do it).

During the haka, the men contort their face, roll their eyes and cry, *"Ka Mate! Ka Mate!"* This is designed to unsettle their opponents and ensure a victory.

Not all haka dances were war dances: some were used to welcome and entertain visitors.

Roll your eyes, waggle your tongue and look fierce to dance the haka.

Belly dancing

This ancient dance originated in the Middle East. Its proper name is *raks sharqui*, meaning 'dance of the East'. In belly dancing, the hips are actually used more than the belly. The head, shoulders and arms are also used. Some people believe that belly dancing was a form of goddess worship. It is still used as a healing dance in parts of North Africa.

Dragon dance

The dragon dance is an important tradition in China. In Chinese culture, the dragon is a rain god, and the dance was originally performed to bring an end to a drought.

This dance is now performed at various festivals, but more as entertainment than for any religious or spiritual purpose.

A colourful dragon is made out of paper stretched over a frame. It has poles attached to the underside, which the performers hold. A dragon can be up to 100 metres (328 feet) long. The performers dance along, raising and lowering the dragon with the poles so that it looks as though it is leaping and diving through the crowd.

Highland dancing

In Scotland, men traditionally took part in special dances as a test of their strength, agility and stamina. These dances were performed at the Highland Games, and were also used by Scottish soldiers as a type of fitness training.

The oldest of the highland dances is the highland fling. This is a dance of celebration, performed after a victory in battle. It is danced over a pair of crossed swords, which may originally have been the sword of the victor and of his defeated adversary.

Belly dancing costumes are heavily embroidered and often have jewels sewn on them. Simple copies can be hired from costume-hire shops.

Further information

Websites

wikipedia.org
Search 'Indian classical dance' and you will find a picture showing lots of different bharata natyam moves being danced.

www.riverdance.com
There are some good video and audio clips on this site.

www.newzealand.com
Learn the moves and words for the traditional haka dance performed by the All Blacks rugby team before an international match.

DVDs, videos and CDs

Irish Dancing Step by Step, Volume I, Olive Hurley
A video that teaches five soft-shoe dances: easy reel, easy jig, easy slip-jig, easy single jig, walls of Limerick.

Irish Dancing Step by Step, Volume 2, Olive Hurley
A video that teaches five hard-shoe dances: treble jig, hornpipe and the traditional set dances, St. Patrick's Day dance, the blackbird.

Manuel Salado – El Baile Flamenco
A collection of DVDs and CDs that introduces the basics of flamenco dancing. For beginners and more experienced dancers.

Dances of India – Learning Bharata Natyam
This DVD includes: salutation, basic positions, hand gestures, warm-up exercises, head movements, eye movements and poses, as well as costumes and make-up.

Note to parents and teachers: every effort has been made by the Publishers to ensure that these websites are suitable for children, that they are of the highest educational value, and that they contain no inappropriate or offensive material. However, because of the nature of the Internet, it is impossible to guarantee that the contents of these sites will not be altered. We strongly advise that Internet access is supervised by a responsible adult.

Dancing is a fun way to get fit, but like any form of physical exercise it has an element of risk, particularly if you are unfit, overweight or suffer from any medical conditions. It is advisable to consult a healthcare professional before beginning any programme of exercise.

Glossary

Adavus The 120 basic steps (movements and poses) of the Indian classical dance bharata natyam.

Aerobic exercise Exercise that improves breathing and circulation.

Baile The element of dance in Spanish flamenco.

Beat The regular pulse in a piece of music. In flamenco dancing, the beat is irregular (see page 16).

Bharata natyam A type of Indian classical dance.

Bollywood A nickname for Mumbai in India, where many Indian musical films are made.

Canto Spanish flamenco singing.

Castanets Wooden discs that are held in the hand and clicked together in time to Spanish flamenco music.

Ceili (pronounced 'kaylee') Irish folk dancing.

Coordination The ability to move different parts of the body together at the same time.

Duende A special inner feeling that inspires flamenco dancers to great performances.

Feis (pronounced 'fesh') Competitions for Irish step dancers.

Fiesta An outdoor party in Spain.

Flamenco A type of rhythmic and passionate dance, which originated in Andalusia in Spain. It is danced on a hard floor, with hard shoes, and involves stamping and clapping.

Gillies Soft shoes with intricate lacing, worn by girls for Irish step dancing.

Guitarra Spanish flamenco guitar-playing.

Haka A Maori dance. Today it is performed by the New Zealand rugby team before international matches.

Hormone A substance produced by the body, which affects the way the body functions.

Improvisation Making up steps as you dance.

Isolations A type of exercise involving moving one part of the body without moving the rest.

Kathak An Indian classical dance.

Palmas Hand clapping in Spanish flamenco dancing.

Rhythm The regular sounds in a piece of music.

Ruffles The gathered pieces of material that decorate traditional flamenco dresses.

Index

First published in 2005 by Franklin Watts,
96 Leonard Street, London EC2A 4XD

Franklin Watts Australia
Level 17/207 Kent Street
Sydney NSW 2000

Copyright © Franklin Watts 2005

Series editor: Rachel Cooke
Art director: Peter Scoulding

**Series designed and created for Franklin
Watts by STOREYBOOKS Ltd.**
Designer: Rita Storey
Editor: Fiona Corbridge
Photography: Tudor Photography, Banbury
Dance consultant: Lucie-Grace Welsman

Picture credits
Corbis/ Robbie Jack p. 9; Corbis Sygma/ Beirne
Brendan p. 21; Corbis/ Reuters/ Arko Datta p. 27.

Cover images: Tudor Photography, Banbury.

Every attempt has been made to clear copyright.
Should there be any inadvertent omissions, please
apply to the publisher for rectification.

All photos posed by models.
Thanks to James Boyce, Kimesha Campbell, Hazel
Hathway, Ricky Healey, Aisha Hussain, Fern
Jelleyman, Charlie Storey and Hannah Storey.

With many thanks to Goody Two Shoes, Rugby,
who supplied all the costumes.

A CIP catalogue record for this book is available
from the British Library.
Dewey number: 792.8
ISBN 0 7496 6349 9
Printed in China